Table of Contents

Introduction 1

Phase 1: Importance of Sponsorship Development 3

Phase 2: The Sponsorship Pitch Deck 12

Phase 3: Sponsorship Tool Kit 31

Conclusion 43

Your guide to understanding and creating
a winning sponsorship strategy

How to Get a
SPONSORSHIP

Non-Profit Edition

Darin Roche

How to Get a Sponsorship
Copyright © 2020 by Darin Roche

All rights reserved. No part of this publication may be reproduced, distributed, or transmitted in any form or by any means, including photocopying, recording, or other electronic or mechanical methods, without the prior written permission of the author, except in the case of brief quotations embodied in critical reviews and certain other non-commercial uses permitted by copyright law.

Tellwell Talent
www.tellwell.ca

ISBN
978-0-2288-3272-0 (Paperback)
978-0-2288-3273-7 (eBook)

Introduction

The sponsorship marketing industry represented more than US$65,000,000 in annual global sales in 2018. This is a staggering number. Would your organization benefit from having a sponsor as part of your fundraising goals? If so, how do you tap into that market? As a non-profit organization, you will need to step back and learn from *The Sponsorship Playbook* that I have created in the following pages.

I have been involved in the sponsorship marketing industry for over 18 years. As a Sponsorship Director for several organizations in the past, I have learned many ways to obtain and maintain relationships with sponsors to keep them coming back year after year on many projects. I am excited to have the opportunity to share my strategy with you to better prepare your organization for winning in the sponsorship marketing industry.

The following pages will help your organization understand the industry, design and tools required in a detailed three-phase approach to sponsorship marketing development. I will take you through the importance of fundraising with sponsors, the creation of a winning sponsorship deck and finally the strategy to implement the tools you will need to start winning in sponsorship.

As non-profit organizations can seek sponsors for many activities and events, for the remainder of the book I will refer to these as "events."

PHASE 1

Importance of Sponsorship Development

Traditional forms of fundraising differ from corporate sponsorship. Understanding the differences will help in the approach you take towards your organization's events that will require sponsorship.

Fundraising is the process of requesting contributions of money from individuals, businesses or charitable organizations. For a long time, typical fundraising consisted of asking for money through donation letters or going "door to door" asking for donations. Children's sports teams will usually have the parents taking different product forms to work or to their family as part of a fundraising campaign. An example might be a raffle for two flights anywhere a certain airline travels. Fundraising is used mostly by non-profit organizations, but newer and unique ways of fundraising have emerged within the for-profit sector as well, for example using online raffle sites. Below is an example of a traditional form of fundraising.

> *A traditional fundraising method is bottle drives for your children's sports teams, Girl Guide cookie drive, or charity auctions. Larger organizations that use similar fundraising methods include the Red Cross, Make A Wish Foundation and Unicef, to name a few. These organizations promote fundraising events each year to help reach their funding goals, which will help them stay in business and continue to spread their message.*

As fundraising involves a donation of money, the benefit to the funder is the opportunity to give back to the community. In some cases, the funder may be offered a donation receipt, which can be used at tax time. Consult with a taxation professional for further details.

Sponsorship is the financial support given towards an event, festival, activity, idea or person in return for equal monetary value of the sponsorship. For example, a sponsor gives $15,000 to a non-profit organization in exchange for receiving $15,000 of value in return.

Three Ways a Company Can Be a Sponsor

Cash Sponsorships

Cash sponsorships are an investment from a company that is interested in supporting your event or organization. They give you a cash investment in return for having their brand promoted at your event, with the promotion worth an equal value.

Media Sponsorships

Media sponsors are financial sponsors that secure advertising for an event, often using a matching funds model. For example:

> *Your organization establishes a partnership with a media company. The media company wishes to do a 50/50 advertising spend. Here is how it works. Your organization spends $2,000 in advertising. A media sponsor will put in an additional $2,000 sponsorship for advertising for a total ad spend of $4,000.*

Both the non-profit and the funder benefit from the ad, which will help to increase awareness and reach for both parties. In return for the new sponsorship of $2,000 that the media sponsor gave, you will provide $2,000 worth of sponsorship benefits, which we will cover in Phase 2.

In-Kind Sponsorships

In this type of sponsorship, goods or services are provided instead of cash in return for equal value. For example:

> *If your organization needs event insurance, you may source a sponsor in that field to work with your organization to offer event insurance at no cost to you in dollars. The value in dollars of insurance is considered in-kind. You will then provide that value in dollars' worth of sponsorship benefits.*

Sources of Revenues for an Event

For an event to be successful, multiple sources of revenue are often needed. Organizations need to understand that sponsorship funding is only one piece. I refer to this as the One-third Approach, as described below:

1. There are many government grants and foundation programs offered throughout the world to assist your organization's sponsorship funding activities. Each country will have its own unique way in which to offer assistance to your organization.

2. The sale of tickets, merchandise, application fees and submission fees are examples of what makes up your organization's program revenue.

It is good practice to visit the cost of these items every two years. A small bump in tickets, fees and submissions can mean more revenue to your bottom line.

3. The third revenue source is sponsorship, which is the financial support given towards an event, festival, activity, idea or person in return for equal monetary value of the sponsorship.

The **One-third Approach** is a protocol that I have used when working with clients to help me analyze the current state of an organization's financial health—what I call its heartbeat. In an ideal scenario, each of the above revenue sources would represent 33.33% of your total budget for your event.

Relying too heavily on government funding and less on program and sponsorship revenue puts your activities in a position of potential failure. Since we know that government funding can be here one year and gone the next without warning, the importance of sponsorship revenue becomes your best ally for your organization's stability and success.

As a good practice, you should analyze your current budget for your activity and break down where the revenue is currently coming from. From here, you will get a snapshot of what needs attention to satisfy the One-third Approach.

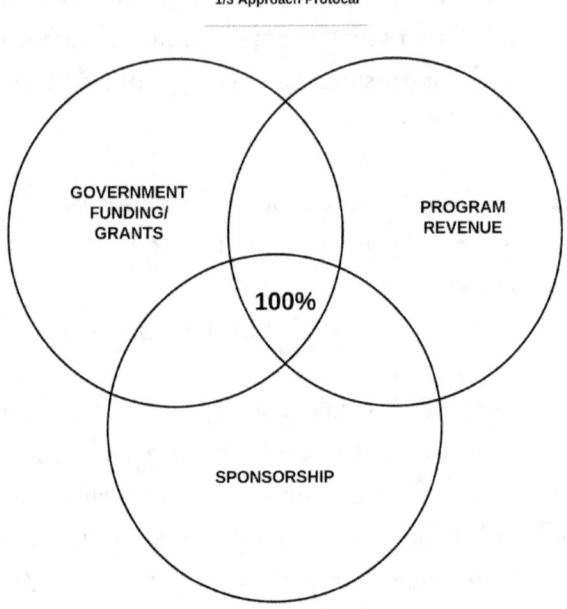

One-third Approach example:

Your event budget $50,000
<u>Made up of:</u>
Government/Foundation Funding $16,666   1/3
Program Revenue $16,666   1/3
Sponsorship Revenue $16,666   1/3

Purpose of Sponsorships

Corporate sponsorships have become one of the fastest growing types of marketing in North America. **Why?** It provides the sponsor with an opportunity to extend their audience reach and offers a competitive advantage by promoting the company's image, values and credibility. Another plus for the sponsor is that they are given the chance to gauge customer response to products immediately, providing they activate their brand within your organization's event.

Additional benefits to the sponsor include:

- Enhanced visibility
- Brand positioning
- Increased awareness
- Media coverage
- Targeted audience exposure

"Partnership before Sponsorship"
~Darin Roche

What's in It for Your Organization?

Let's discuss what a sponsorship means to your organization. Having sponsors invested in your event allows your organization to continue providing community programming while also paying the bills! Funding generated by sponsorships usually goes directly to your programming, and at times you will use this funding to keep your doors open.

Attaching sponsors will help get your concept off the ground! All of your organization's events cost money, and sponsorship helps with those costs.

It's not only about the cost, however. When you have sponsors, you are instantly adding value to your organization's activities. Once you have sourced a quality number of sponsors for your activity, you also get to take advantage of new reach as well. Multiple sponsors drive more eyes and additional interest to your event, which will likely lead to additional program revenue in return.

> **TIP!** *You can have too many sponsors for your event; I call it "Logo Soup." A quality number will be gauged by how large your event is and over how many days. You want to avoid the sponsor takeover effect. Quality sponsors equal additional revenue!*

Impact of Sponsorship

The social and economical impacts of sponsorships can create a solid foundation for your organization's cause, which can bring communities together around your events and also the mission and purpose. Sponsorship also lends itself to bringing two brands (identities) together for wider exposure.

How do you measure the success of your sponsorship development? Here are three ways:

1. **Understand Your Audience**

    Who is your audience? How does the audience engage with your event? What is the demographic footprint, such as how many people will attend, are you skewed male or female, what is the average age of your attendees and finally does your event complement the audience you have designed your event for?

2. **Understand the Collaboration**

   Solid sponsorships are built on relationships. Understanding how the collaboration will work between your event and the sponsor is critical. Both your organization and the sponsor should understand each other's business—this is where synergy will be born. Finally, know what both parties are bringing into the relationship from value to potential reach.

3. **Provide Accurate Data**

   Capturing accurate data can be one of the best ways to pitch your event to a sponsor. It gives them a good idea of who and what their investment will immediately impact. Measuring a sponsor's impact can be accomplished by compiling information such as social media, actual attendance numbers, newsletters, logo representation and sponsor feedback.

PHASE 2

The Sponsorship Pitch Deck

A sponsorship pitch deck is a document that outlines your organization's specific event that you are seeking sponsorship for. The pitch deck includes all of the necessary components needed to present to a sponsor with the hopes of securing a sponsorship deal.

The first step to creating a winning pitch deck is to understand the purpose of why you need one in the first place.

Purpose of a Sponsor Pitch Deck

Now that you have conceived an event for your organization, it is time to develop the pitch deck, but why do you need one?

Your pitch deck will present the following items to a potential sponsor:

1. **Structure**

   Taking the time to understand and create a pitch deck shows your potential sponsor that you have put a considerable amount of time in preparing for your event, but it also shows the sponsor that you have a given structure to the event and an understanding of what your event is all about.

2. **Value**

   When you have a structure to any event, you are adding value for your potential sponsor. For example, you have a potential sponsor asking you for additional information about your event, and instead of an email, you send her a version of your most current sponsor pitch deck for her review. The email will detail everything her business needs to know about your event—from activation, title partnership, investment levels and benefits. They in fact are able to understand your event from a higher perspective.

   The sponsorship pitch deck becomes a professional, integral part of your overall sales approach to landing a new sponsorship.

3. Professionalism

Now that you have structure and value, what does that equal? *Professionalism!* You have now just resonated with a potential sponsor in the most formal way possible—with professionalism. No matter which way you look at the sponsorship industry, whether in-kind or cash investments, they are a business transaction. An investment from a potential sponsor is very important to your organization but also the sponsor as well. Therefore, having a professional pitch deck will increase your chances of moving to the next step, an agreement!

Building Your Pitch Deck

It's time to roll up your sleeves and get down in the dirt! Building your pitch deck takes time, energy and thought. There are a number of components that make up a pitch deck. But before we get to those, it is important to lay the groundwork that your pitch deck will be built on. Here are the components of a strong foundation:

1. Know Your Audience

To get started in the design, you need to know who your target audience is as well as a small list of potential sponsors to approach.

2. **Target Market**

   Once you have established your event, you will need to know who your target market will be. This will be important to know as it allows you to hone in on how the overall pitch deck will look and feel. Consider the age, sex, income, gender and any other target identifier of this market. You will be asked—trust me!

3. **Community or Corporate**

   Creating a pitch deck for a community concept or a corporate event can change the entire landscape of your deck. For example, community-based investment levels may include philanthropic benefits, while corporate-based levels will include a variety of benefits associated with the value of the sponsorship.

The Title Page

Before we dive into the components that make up a sponsor pitch deck, we need a title page, not just any title page, but one with a purpose.

Your title page will need to have an image that fills the page from whatever design platform you or your graphic designer will use. This image should represent a snapshot of a previous event you have done, and, if possible, it should show the audience the feel of the event and the scope. Once you have selected the image, the title of your event is positioned front and centre on the page. Right underneath the title you will want to create the value proposition or brand message in a few words. Here are two examples:

Inspire. Motivate. Move.

*Partnering through the connective
power of community*

Lastly, if your organization has any current partnerships that relate to the event you are putting on, place their logos on the bottom right or left. These partnerships may be a key ingredient to a potential new sponsor.

Now let's break down the components for the sponsorship pitch deck.

Component 1. About Your Organization

To get your pitch deck started, your organization will need to create an "about" paragraph, the lead for your pitch deck. This paragraph should contain a quick description of your organization, your core values and why you conduct events.

The key to a sponsorship pitch deck is to keep it short and to the point—less is more! Your potential sponsor does not have the time to read pages and pages of content about your organization. It is best if you can describe your organization in 200 to 400 words maximum.

The idea is not to write a story but to give the best representation of your organization to gain a potential sponsor's interest to keep reviewing.

Component 2. Activation in Sponsorship

Working in the sponsorship marketing industry, I know that one of the most important advances is how you will create an experience for your potential sponsors during your event. Developing and compiling a list of activation concepts for your sponsors will become extremely critical.

Activation in sponsorship is to create a series of actions for your sponsor that will help promote their brand on site, while also offering attendees the chance to get close to their favourite brands.

A few examples of an activation concept include:

- Hydration station branded with sponsor logo
- Smartphone charging station branded with sponsor logo
- Interactive installations such as a Twitter or Instagram wall
- Photo booth branded with sponsor logo

The sponsor will see even more value when you bring them activation concepts to coincide with the rest of the pitch deck. Be creative with this process.

Let's break down a few more activation concepts with greater detail.

Wi-Fi Login: Almost every event will have a Wi-Fi login setup available to all sponsors and attendees of your event. Make this login screen an activation by offering a company logo that will be placed on the landing page of the Wi-Fi login. For example, "Wi-Fi brought to you by [name of sponsor]."

Street Pole Banners: In some cities, there may be an opportunity to reach out to your local business association for the opportunity to allow you to put up street pole banners with your event logo as well as a sponsor's logo. You can charge a separate sponsorship fee for this opportunity.

Volunteer Program: Sourcing a company to be a volunteer program sponsor can generate all sorts of ideas and concepts. Offering a company to have their logo displayed on volunteer shirts creates a great feel-good story. There are many companies that value this type of activation as the most important one. Not only does it provide exposure, it also promotes community.

You could also have that same sponsor put on the pre-event volunteer reception as a way to rally the volunteers together, have fun and make introductions ahead of your event.

Receptions and Galas: Establish a VIP reception or gala and consider offering it up to a sponsor as an activation. Having a sponsored reception allows the sponsor to work with you on how they wish to expose their brand during the reception.

> **TIP!** *Try to ensure that the focus of the reception is not just about brand exposure for your sponsor as it may be considered cheeky. The right amount of exposure with an activation like this could be pull-up banner signage, colour-specific lighting around the room, a speaking opportunity and subtle branding throughout.*

Pop-Up Tents: If you have a good amount of room within your event, create the opportunity to have a branded pop-up tent for your sponsor. Allow them to promote with product samples, merchandise, swag and anything else that could generate exposure within this space. An appropriate tent size could be 10 x 10 feet.

> **TIP!** *It is always a nice gesture to your attendees to have a "no-roaming" clause for this type of activation. This clause limits the sponsor to a five-foot extension of their tent to talk to people, put in place to mitigate roaming around in an open forum at your event.*

Red Carpet: It's time to roll out the red carpet to create an experience for your event. Offer a sponsor the chance to collaborate with you on a red-carpet experience through contesting or social media posting. Sponsors will enjoy the opportunity to have their logo sprinkled on a 10- x16-foot backdrop—the perfect setting for photographs.

Although red is the standard color for a "red carpet," you could also arrange for any color carpet designed with the sponsor's scheme in mind or a white carpet with their logo on it. The possibilities are endless!

These are only a few activation designs you can offer a sponsor. Have fun creating your own or use the above list to get you started.

Remember, you may choose to attach a separate dollar value to each activation or incorporate the dollar value within the benefits you will create in Component 4.

Component 3. Infographics

The second most important segment in a pitch deck is infographics. An infographic is a visual representation of your organization's ethos, which is your organization's core beliefs and aspirations. An infographic is designed to complement statistics, social, reach and marketing data that a sponsor can visualize through graphics.

If you do not have the collection of data above, it should be researched and solidified within your group prior to the design process. An example of an infographic can be found at *www.sponsorshipplaybook.com/infographic*.

There are many infographic-maker platforms on the internet. The three that I use most are Canva, Venngage and Piktochart.

Component 4. Creating Benefits

Sponsorships can be created for different levels of giving, such as Bronze, Silver, Gold and Platinum levels, as you may have seen for accomplishments at some point in your career. Each level would give the sponsor different benefits. Creating these pitch deck levels and benefits is time-consuming, but I will share a couple of tips that will help you along the way.

Benefits for your pitch deck are items offered to your sponsor for sponsoring your event that is part of the value return on their sponsorship investment.

My suggestion is that you list all of the benefits you plan on offering your potential sponsor. These benefits to a sponsor can include logo recognition, online recognition, videos, social and media options, among many others. Below, I will detail several ideas to get you started!

In the sponsorship marketing industry, you can design and offer your sponsor many benefit combinations. It is always a safe bet to offer what I call the "standard benefits" that most organizations use when creating a pitch deck.

Here are a few sample benefits you may want to start with:

Website: Include a sponsor's logo on your website. Consult with your sponsor on the potential placement of the logo. I will normally place a sponsor logo as a header or leaderboard on an organization's website or even off to one side with a direct link to the sponsor's website.

Program Guide: A great benefit to include is logo recognition in your event program guide. A program guide is usually a magazine-style publication of your entire event that you give out to your audience. It has information about the event's hours and program, supporters and advertisements, to name a few.

What you decide to offer your sponsor could depend on which level of sponsorship they invest in. A sponsor who invests in higher levels might also receive the opportunity to write a welcome message in the guide along with their logo. Placement of the logo and welcome message will depend on how you have laid out your program guide.

Advertisement: A great way to add more value to your program guide is to offer your sponsor an advertisement in the program guide. The larger the investment, the larger the advertisement size. Consider offering a full-page advertisement on the front and back covers of the program guide.

> **TIP!** *A back-cover (full-page) advertisement performs better in most cases than the front cover, which allows you to sell it as a higher investment.*

Posters: Most event organizers will create an event poster that will be placed usually on lamp poles, store bulletin boards, coffee shops and many more high-traffic areas where the poster will be been. Offering logo representation for your sponsor on the event poster creates a visual credibility to other potential sponsors as well as to your audience.

Positioning of your sponsor logos on the event poster typically lands on the bottom of the poster, as a leaderboard-style design.

> **TIP!** *Place sponsor logos from left to right with the highest level of sponsorship first.*

Sponsor Banner: A great way to recognize your event sponsors is to create sponsor banners. The design of the banners should list sponsors from the highest level of sponsorship down to the lowest. Using your sponsor's logos is the best method for recognition by all viewers. The banners, once designed, can be sent to the printers to be placed in a pull-up banner sign. Place the banners in strategic foot traffic areas to offer the best chance for maximum visibility.

Social Media*:* We cannot forget about social media promotion. Incorporate a daily e-blast through your social channels, including tweets, Instagram posts and Facebook posts. Strategize with your sponsors to offer a product of the day or discounted offer around social media posting or following. The combinations are endless for what you can design as a social media strategy with your sponsors. Have fun and be creative!

As standard benefits are needed for your pitch deck, niche benefits should also be considered. A niche benefit goes one step further on creativity. Below, I have listed several niche benefits that can be included in your pitch deck:

- Speaking opportunity
- 30-second video clip
- Unique sponsor-branded products
- VIP reception
- Logo recognition on tickets
- Special announcements
- On-site branding
- Social media walls

Component 5. Creating and Naming Levels

Now that you have created a list of benefits, it is now time to establish your event levels that your potential sponsor will have to decide upon.

Just so that we are on the same page, you will have seen levels named in a pitch deck from a prior experience. Typically, they are listed as follows:

- Title
- Signature
- Major
- Platinum
- Gold
- Silver
- Bronze
- Supporter
- Community

These level names are most widely used in most pitch decks and proposals. If your organization seeks a new way of naming levels, try to create level names based on what your event is about.

As an example, if I was putting on an annual fishing derby that had an expo attached to it, I may design the naming of my levels as such:

- Tuna
- Halibut

- Salmon
- Trout
- Bass
- Perch

Just to be clear, the Tuna level would be the highest sponsor level, while Perch would be the lowest sponsor level. Take the time to create unique level names. If nothing else, they will receive a few chuckles!

Let's put it all together. You now should have all benefits listed and level names. For the highest level of investment, place all of your benefits under that level. As you work backwards, reduce the benefits by two or three for each level. Once complete, you should have your levels and benefits organized. Great job!

Component 6. Level Investment

Now that you have secured your levels and benefits, it is time to attach an investment to each level. To figure out what investment you should attach to each level, you will need to consider the following items:

Budget for the Event

If your organization hasn't done so yet, now is a great time to produce an event budget. As an example, if your budget is $10,000, your levels will be priced accordingly. If your budget is $100,000, your levels will be set higher for each. Remember back when we discussed the One-third Approach? It would be ideal to use that model as you prepare to place dollar values on each level. Here is how it works:

1. Identify your budget
2. Subtract your government or foundation funding
3. Subtract projected program revenue

Once you are secure with the numbers above as potential and secured revenue, you will be left with a number that you will need to satisfy through sponsorship. This is your starting point. The amount required from sponsorship is then broken down for each level. It's a good practice to use a capped system for your levels, such as one sponsorship is available at Title, three available at Gold and so on. Using this method, you will be able to capture where your sponsorships will need to be made up from.

Length of Your Event

The longer your event runs, the more it costs, the larger the amount of investment from sponsors you will need. If your event runs only a couple of days, you might be able to get away with smaller investment level values.

Scope of Your Event

If your event is a smaller, community-based event with a lower budget, you may lower the price for each level.

Conversely, if your event is a large-scale festival or a three- to five-day conference, your investment dollar levels will be higher to compensate for what you will need in sponsorship.

> **TIP!** Consider creating a Community Partners program, offering $250 to $500 sponsorships in return for logo recognition in the program guide as well as an opportunity for each partner to promote their support by placing a "Proud to Support" window cling on their shop window. A window cling is a digital print advertisement that uses static electricity to cling to a window, which means you can put it o, and peel it off with ease!

You will be surprised at how quickly these small dollar amounts of items add up. Remember, "it's not how you get there, just get there!"

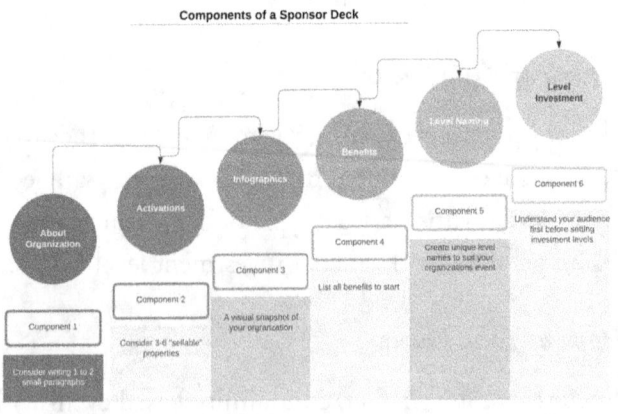

How to Organize Your Pitch Deck

It's now time to take all of this information and look at getting your newly created pitch deck ready for the light of day.

You have created your pitch deck within your platform of choice. Now you need to organize it before it's ready to hit the street. Here's how to set it up and arrange the order of it:

- Title Page of Event
- About Organization
- Activation Opportunities
- Infographics
- Levels and Benefits
- Contact Information

The Setup

It is important to create your pitch deck as separate pages in the design platform you are using to create it. Having separate pages enables you to pull and send a quick one-pager from the pitch deck to a potential sponsor upon their request. The reality is some potential sponsors will request some basic information as a starting point. Typically, I will not send the entire pitch deck at this time but only one of the pages, usually the infographics page.

You will want to save your pitch deck as a PDF file. Remember that a content-heavy document also means a larger file size. I recommend saving a second version in a reduced file format, which you can do in Adobe Acrobat or Apple's Preview application.

PHASE 3

Sponsorship Tool Kit

Every sponsorship plan requires a tool kit to be a winner! The following tools and strategies will be necessary for your organization as a starting point. I recommend a few planning sessions with your team to produce the following items:

Develop a Target List of Potential Sponsors

A target list will help you get started in identifying and eventually prospecting the right sponsor for your event. Target lists should always be coupled with a contact list to enable you to keep track of your progress. Go to *www.sponsorshipplaybook.com/tracking* to download a template of the tracking document I have created for this book.

A great way to start developing your target list is to research similar events to see which companies are sponsoring them. If you are researching online, go to their website and search for keywords like partners, sponsors or community involvement. Hitting on those links will likely take you to a page that lists all of their sponsors.

From that research, you get a sense of the type of companies that are sponsoring an event similar to yours. Then either reach out directly to them or source similar companies to use in your targeting.

Prospect the Target List

Now that you have identified and compiled your target list, prospecting is next. Prospecting is the start of the sales process whereby you start to reach out to identified potential sponsors in your target list. Your goal here is to start a narrative around your event with the potential sponsor. There are a number of ways in which you can approach prospecting, but try these first:

Cold Calling

If you are OK with being on the phone and are comfortable discussing your organization's event to a potential sponsor, start dialing! Picking up the phone is a direct method of telemarketing that in most cases is very successful. Try to be short and to the point, not taking up too much of a potential sponsor's time nor getting into too much detail right away.

What you're trying to deliver is an elevator pitch (what I call your You-Pitch) of who, what and why you are reaching out to a potential sponsor. The goal of your You-Pitch is to get to a face-to-face meeting or Zoom call in which the initial details will be discussed. Grab their interest, and set up a second, more in-depth meeting. Here is a sample script you can try:

"Good day!

I am looking to speak with [Name].

Hi, my name is [Name] and I am the Sponsorship Director for [Organization]. We have launched a new event called [Name]. If I could take a few moments to discuss the reason for this call that would be great!"

If you get a yes: start your pitch!

If you get a no: *"I understand. Perhaps I could take your email and send you some information about our event."*

In both cases end with: *"Thank you very much for your time. I hope to talk again soon!"*

Email

Email marketing can be very successful when trying to attract a potential sponsor to your event. Done correctly, an email represents a warm approach as long as you send an appropriate message. You will need to craft an email that does not have an open-ended response from a potential sponsor, that is, do not ask a question that can be answered with no or yes.

Using this method of prospecting requires some work and preparation. Here is a sample script you can try:

> *"Good day [Name],*
>
> *I hope all is well with you. I am the Sponsorship Director for [Organization].*
>
> *Would you be the person I could start a narrative with regarding community sponsorship? We have launched [Event] and would like to know more about how you might have sponsored similar events in the past, and possibly what your process is for accepting sponsorship requests.*
>
> *Thank you very much, and I look forward to your reply in advance!"*

Online

I have spent many hours prospecting for new sponsors for many events over the last 10 years. One method that is becoming a very integral prospecting tool is LinkedIn. Using LinkedIn as a prospecting tool cuts your prospecting time in half!

LinkedIn comes free for a standard user, but once you unlock the subscription accounts (Premium Subscriptions), it becomes a whole new ball game! I strongly believe that an investment of $100 per month is worth discovering the decision-makers who can support your event!

LinkedIn is one of many online prospecting tools you can use to enhance your efforts. Go ahead and try them to get a feel for what works for you and your organization.

Below is a sample script I use when prospecting via LinkedIn:

> *"Good day, [Name],*
>
> *I hope all is well with you. I am hoping you might be the person I could speak to with regard to Canadian-based sponsorships?*
>
> *I am interested in starting a narrative with your company about [Event] that I am the Sponsorship*

Director for. I am seeking a company such as [Company] for a potential sponsorship opportunity. What is the best way to connect with you?"

Networking

One of the more fun and energetic ways of prospecting is networking! Plan to go to other events, festivals or community gatherings. Most likely, sponsors will be present. Take the time to introduce yourself to a sponsor and have your You-Pitch ready. If a sponsor you are talking to is eager and interested, you may be able to strike up a quick conversation regarding the opportunity.

You are there to network, not to ramble on for 30 to 60 minutes about your event. The potential sponsor will guide you when the timing is right through the conversation. Have fun!

You-Pitch

You should allow for 30 seconds for a You-Pitch. Here's what to include:

> Who you are: *your current title*
> Where you have been: *a very quick history*
> What you are best at: *key competencies and accomplishments*
> What you are currently working on: *details of your new project*

What you are looking for and why: *your goal from the introduction*

Go to *www.sponsorshipplaybook.com/youpitch* to listen to a sample!

To help you see the overall sales process for obtaining sponsorships, I have created a sponsorship sales process flowchart for you to follow each step of the way.

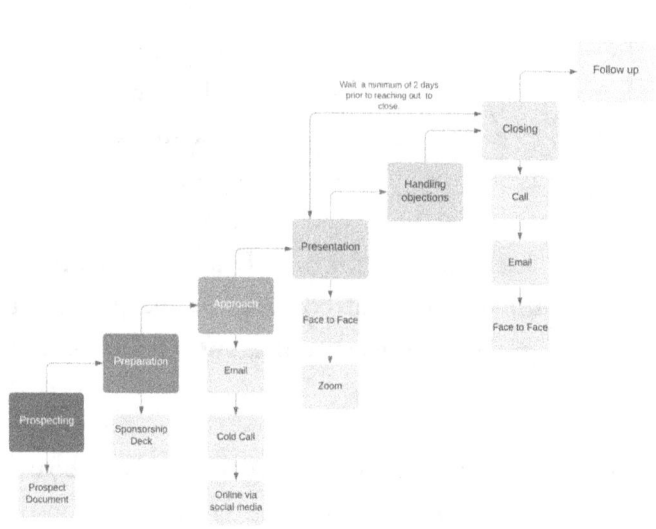

The Sponsorship Playbook Sales Process

Tool Up

There are three additional documents you will need to complete your sponsorship tool kit. Let's review what you now have in the tool kit so far:

- Identified your event
- Created a winning Sponsorship Pitch Deck
- Created a Target List
- Created a Prospect flow

You are doing great! So, let's now discuss the final three tools you will need to implement your sponsorship strategy.

Sponsor Agreement

After you have done the hard work of connecting with a potential sponsor, provided the pitch deck, arranged a face-to-face meeting and a few back-and-forth calls later, you ask for the business's sponsorship! The sponsor has accepted your pitch and is interested in moving forward. Exciting, right? **There is a certain feeling of accomplishment and confidence the minute a sponsor agrees to sponsor your event—it's amazing!** But what do you do next?

Your organization may have a legal team or a board member who is a lawyer. It is time to create your sponsor agreement.

The sponsor agreement will close the loop on your new sponsorship deal. It contains important information of the overall agreement, including deadlines, materials, logos, swag and items that will be needed to sign off on.

I have broken the sponsor agreement down into four main elements:

Sponsor Information

It is always a good idea to start your sponsor agreement with the sponsor's contact information as you will need it for reference later on in the fulfillment process.

Level and Benefits

List the level commitment and benefits that you agreed upon. Once you have included these, you will want to also lay out the agreed upon activations as well. Everything that lives in this portion of the agreement is information that you will have to fulfill on closer to and during your event.

Fulfillment Details

Once you completely fill out the sponsor agreement, the details listed within the document will need to move to the fulfillment stage. Fulfillment comes into play a few weeks out from your event and during the event.

At the time you start filling out your fulfillment document, you will need to create some pre-event deadlines and elements for your sponsors, such as dates for receiving logos, marketing material, signage, advertisements and swag. The number of deadlines will depend on your event's size and scope.

One last but important date that you will need to consider is the sponsor lock date. This is the date that you will no longer take on sponsors as your event is approaching. The reason for a lock date is that you will run out of production time for all of the elements needed to fulfill for your sponsor.

Go to *www.sponsorshipplaybook.com/fulfillment* to download a template for your fulfillment document.

Payment Terms

You will need to establish terms for payment from your sponsor. I suggest the standard 60 days from the date of the agreement. Once the sponsor agreement is signed, it is common protocol to prepare an invoice and send it right away. Oftentimes, sponsors will want to pay you based on their current fiscal year.

Visibility Report

Often missed but not required is a visibility report for your sponsor. A visibility report is a document that is put together post-event that has in it all of the agreed upon benefits, activations and photos that were promised to your sponsor. It is a way for you to prove that what was agreed upon was fulfilled. Typically the report is sent within 30 days after the event. It may seem like additional work, but this piece of documentation is considered basic to relationship building.

A visibility report offers valuable insight into the success of your event as well as confirms that your organization completed all required elements from the sponsor agreement. The report will detail what was promised and executed.

The visibility report delivers photos, social statistics, program guide advertisement samples and any other relevant information supporting your fulfillment and agreement details. The report shows that you followed through on your proposed benefits to your sponsor and what was agreed to.

Your visibility report should be organized as follows:

- Title Page
- About your organization (*yes, again!*)
- All of the statistics (*social, attendance, media*)
- Photos of sponsor signage and all relevant elements
- Photos of program guide placements, contesting, e-newsletters
- All mentions of the sponsor

When you provide this report, it will lead you to the very first conversation for the following year. It's a great time to end the conversation with something like this: "We have lots of time to discuss and collaborate together on what next year looks like for our partnership."

Quick Hits

Here is a list of a few quick hits or bullet points that can help you navigate the sponsorship process in order to move closer to a new sponsorship deal:

- Seek three-year sponsorship agreements
- Set the sponsor lock date to no less than four weeks out from your event
- Always offer more value than the investment from the sponsor
- If a sponsor asks for some brief information, send the Infographics Page
- Reach out to your sponsor a minimum of three or four times per year
- Have a volunteer/staff member photograph all sponsor details promised
- Assign one person on your staff to handle sponsor questions during the event
- Request sponsor pull-up sign banners two to three weeks out in the event of a shipping mishap
- Make the effort to greet and talk to sponsors during the entire event
- Sponsors generally close budgets for the following year by November, so your best chance to position your event for sponsorship starts in late spring, goes through the summer and ends in October.

Conclusion

Sponsorship fund development is a daily hustle. It deserves the full attention required to see your goals through to fruition. Sponsorship should not be pushed to the bottom of the task pile any longer. It needs to become your number one ally for continued success.

It would not be fair for me to leave you without mentioning this. As sponsorships are based on relationships that lead to partnerships, it is very important to consider the core values and beliefs of both your organization and the sponsor. Bringing on sponsors that may not share the same values could result in a poor partnership, which tarnishes the relationship and could lead to a poor sponsorship.

If your organization has followed this playbook, you will begin to see results. Enjoy the process, enjoy the chase and enjoy the rewards of winning in sponsorship.

www.ingramcontent.com/pod-product-compliance
Lightning Source LLC
LaVergne TN
LVHW011900060526
838200LV00054B/4448